6th Grade Math Workbook
Introduction to Integers

Speedy Publishing LLC
40 E. Main St. #1156
Newark, DE 19711
www.speedypublishing.com

Adding Integers

Simple addition of integers. Solve the following.

1. (-14) + 23 = ______

2. 4 + (-22) = ______

3. (-16) + (-17) = ______

4. 26 + 28 = ______

5. 17 + (-4) = ______

6. 24 + (-7) = ______

7. 17 + (-28) = ______

8. (-20) + (-13) = ______

9. (-1) + 4 = ______

10. (-13) + (-18) = ______

11. (-11) + 29 = ______

12. (-11) + (-14) = ______

13. 0 + (-20) = ______

14. 6 + 13 = ______

15. 22 + 28 = ______

16. (-23) + (-25) = ______

17. (-1) + (-15) = ______

18. (-12) + 13 = ______

19. 23 + 23 = ______

20. 9 + 13 = ______

21. 6 + (-14) = ______

22. (-10) + (-8) = ______

23. (-2) + (-13) = ______

24. 3 + 5 = ______

25. 6 + (-8) = ______

26. 1 + (-18) = ______

27. (-27) + (-14) = ______

28. (-2) + 4 = ______

29. (-24) + 30 = ______

30. (-17) + 10 = ______

31. (-30) + (-7) = ______

32. 12 + (-26) = ______

Missing addend problems. Solve the following.

1. $\_\_\_ + (-6) = -8$

2. $\_\_\_ + 5 = -5$

3. $(-5) + \_\_\_ = -2$

4. $\_\_\_ + 10 = 0$

5. $\_\_\_ + (-9) = -17$

6. $\_\_\_ + (-2) = 0$

7. $0 + \_\_\_ = -7$

8. $(-6) + \_\_\_ = 1$

9. $(-9) + \_\_\_ = -12$

10. $\_\_\_ + (-8) = -14$

11. $7 + \_\_\_ = -2$

12. $\_\_\_ + (-2) = -10$

13. $(-3) + \_\_\_ = 5$

14. $1 + \_\_\_ = -8$

15. $\_\_\_ + 7 = 1$

16. $(-2) + \_\_\_ = -3$

17. $(-10) + \_\_\_ = -18$

18. $(-2) + \_\_\_ = 6$

19. $\_\_\_ + (-5) = -11$

20. $(-8) + \_\_\_ = -12$

21. $\_\_\_ + (-3) = 6$

22. $\_\_\_ + (-2) = -10$

23. $(-10) + \_\_\_ = -2$

24. $\_\_\_ + 5 = -1$

25. $\_\_\_ + (-2) = 8$

26. $\_\_\_ + (-6) = -16$

27. $(-6) + \_\_\_ = 0$

28. $\_\_\_ + (-3) = 4$

29. $\_\_\_ + (-5) = 0$

30. $6 + \_\_\_ = 2$

31. $10 + \_\_\_ = 0$

32. $\_\_\_ + 8 = 1$

33. $(-4) + \_\_\_ = -2$

34. $(-10) + \_\_\_ = -18$

35. (–10) + ___ = –16

36. (–2) + ___ = –11

37. 7 + ___ = 3

38. ___ + (–1) = 4

39. (–4) + ___ = 6

40. 9 + ___ = 8

41. (–3) + ___ = 2

42. 0 + ___ = –1

43. ___ + 2 = –1

44. ___ + 10 = 7

45. ___ + (–8) = –8

46. 4 + ___ = 2

Subtracting Integers

Simple subtraction of integers. Solve the following.

1. (-18) – 3 = ______

2. 29 – (-22) = ______

3. (-19) – 9 = ______

4. 10 – 3 = ______

5. 26 – (-3) = ______

6. (-11) – (-16) = ______

7. (-1) – (-1) = ______

8. 6 – 14 = ______

9. (-11) – 14 = ______

10. 13 – (-22) = ______

11. 23 – (-24) = ______

12. (-1) – (-15) = ______

13. 23 – 10 = ______

14. (-15) – (-7) = ______

15. (-10) – (-26) = ______

16. (-12) – (-19) = ______

17. 2 – (-10) = ______

18. 9 – 28 = ______

19. (-8) – (-22) = ______

20. (-22) – 6 = ______

21. 16 – 11 = ______

22. (-21) – 19 = ______

23. (-18) – (-15) = ______

24. 25 – (-16) = ______

25. 26 – 23 = ______

26. 25 – 20 = ______

27. 17 – 1 = ______

28. 5 – (-14) = ______

29. 22 – (-22) = ______

30. (-23) – 8 = ______

31. 22 – 17 = ______

32. (-30) – (-20) = ______

Missing minuend/subtrahend problems.
Solve the following.

1. (-6) – ______ = (-9)

2. 0 – ______ = 2

3. (-3) – ______ = 4

4. 6 – ______ = (-2)

5. ______ – (-10) = 0

6. (-10) – ______ = (-16)

7. 3 – ______ = (-3)

8. ______ – 7 = (-7)

9. 8 – ______ = 3

10. ______ – 9 = (-6)

11. (-5) – ______ = (-14)

12. 4 – ______ = 12

13. 4 – ______ = (-6)

14. ______ – 0 = 5

15. (-8) – ______ = (-14)

16. ______ – 6 = (-9)

17. (-2) – ______ = (-8)

18. ______ – (-9) = 6

19. 5 – ______ = 6

20. ______ – 10 = (-15)

21. ______ – (-10) = 1

22. ______ – (-1) = 1

23. ______ – 4 = (-8)

24. ______ – (-9) = 14

25. ______ – 4 = (-4)

26. ______ – (-10) = 15

27. ______ – 5 = (-4)

28. ______ – (-9) = 11

29. (-8) – ______ = (-5)

30. ______ – 1 = 9

31. ______ – 4 = 5

32. (-8) – ______ = 2

33. ______ – 3 = (-3)

34. (-10) – ______ = (-6)

35. 5 − ______ = 9

36. ______ − 8 = (-11)

37. 7 − ______ = 13

38. 4 − ______ = (-3)

39. ______ − 7 = (-16)

40. 10 − ______ = 5

41. ______ − 1 = (-5)

42. 10 − ______ = 1

43. (-3) − ______ = 6

44. (-6) − ______ = (-10)

45. ______ − (-4) = 6

46. 4 − ______ = (-2)

Mixed addition & subtraction of integers

Solve the following.

1. (-6) – 20 = ______

2. 4 + 4 = ______

3. (-18) + 3 = ______

4. 6 + (-6) = ______

5. 7 + 0 = ______

6. (-12) – (-9) = ______

7. (-1) – 9 = ______

8. 11 – (-18) = ______

9. $(-18) + 2 =$ ______

10. $6 - 20 =$ ______

11. $17 - 20 =$ ______

12. $(-6) + (-4) =$ ______

13. $(-5) + 8 =$ ______

14. $15 + (-10) =$ ______

15. $3 + 1 =$ ______

16. $(-17) + 14 =$ ______

17. $(-16) - (-20) =$ ______

18. $(-14) + 15 =$ ______

19. $16 - 0 =$ ______

20. $0 + (-2) =$ ______

21. (-19) + (-1) = ______

22. (-16) + 17 = ______

23. 8 – 6 = ______

24. 3 – (-14) = ______

25. 16 + 12 = ______

26. (-19) – 3 = ______

27. (-14) – (-13) = ______

28. (-6) – 13 = ______

29. (-6) – (-1) = ______

30. 18 – 6 = ______

31. (-12) – (-11) = ______

32. 4 + (-15) = ______

Integer Multiplication

Simple multiplication of integers. Solve the following.

1. 10 × (-4) = ______

2. (-19) × (-9) = ______

3. 7 × 9 = ______

4. (-9) × (-16) = ______

5. 9 × (-13) = ______

6. 11 × (-1) = ______

7. 4 × 16 = ______

8. (-2) × 11 = ______

9. 15 × (-9) = ______

10. (-9) × 15 = ______

11. 1 × 7 = ______

12. 2 × (-11) = ______

13. (-12) × 4 = ______

14. (-1) × (-5) = ______

15. 6 × 2 = ______

16. 5 × 10 = ______

17. 4 × (-8) = ______

18. 8 × 3 = ______

19. (-7) × 20 = ______

20. 3 × 17 = ______

Integer Division

Simple division of integers. Solve the following.

1. $36 \div 2 =$ ______

2. $100 \div 2 =$ ______

3. $0 \div (-6) =$ ______

4. $(-88) \div (-8) =$ ______

5. $80 \div 5 =$ ______

6. $22 \div 2 =$ ______

7. $35 \div 5 =$ ______

8. $16 \div 2 =$ ______

9. $93 \div 3 =$ ______

10. $(-63) \div (-7) =$ ______

11. $36 \div 9 =$ ______

12. $12 \div 2 =$ ______

13. $(-81) \div 9 =$ ______

14. $12 \div (-6) =$ ______

15. $70 \div 2 =$ ______

16. $52 \div 4 =$ ______

17. $90 \div 10 =$ ______

18. $60 \div (-6) =$ ______

19. $(-64) \div (-4) =$ ______

20. $32 \div 2 =$ ______

Adding Integers

1. 9
2. -18
3. -33
4. 54
5. 13
6. 17
7. -11
8. -33
9. 3
10. -31
11. 18
12. -25
13. -20
14. 19
15. 50
16. -48
17. -16
18. 1
19. 46
20. 22
21. -8
22. -18
23. -15
24. 8
25. -2
26. -17
27. -41
28. 2
29. 6
30. -7
31. -37
32. -14

Missing Addend

1. (−2)
2. (−10)
3. 3
4. (−10)
5. (−8)
6. 2
7. (−7)
8. 7
9. (−3)
10. (−6)
11. (−9)
12. (−8)
13. 8
14. (−9)
15. (−6)
16. (−1)
17. (−8)
18. 8
19. (−6)
20. (−4)
21. 9
22. (−8)
23. 8
24. (−6)
25. 10
26. (−10)
27. 6
28. 7
29. 5
30. (−4)
31. (−10)
32. (−7)

33. 2

34. (−8)

35. (−6)

36. (−9)

37. (−4)

38. 5

39. 10

40. (−1)

41. 5

42. (−1)

43. (−3)

44. (−3)

45. 0

46. (−2)

Subtracting Integers

1. -21

2. 51

3. -28

4. 7

5. 29

6. 5

7. 0

8. -8

9. -25

10. 35

11. 47

12. 14

13. 13

14. -8

15. 16

16. 7

17. 12

18. -19

19. 14

20. -28

21. 5

22. -40

23. -3

24. 41

25. 3

26. 5

27. 16

28. 19

29. 44

30. -31

31. 5

32. -10

Missing Minuend/Subtrahend

1. 3

2. (-2)

3. (-7)

4. 8

5. (-10)

6. 6

7. 6

8. 0

9. 5

10. 3

11. 9

12. (-8)

13. 10

14. 5

15. 6

16. (-3)

17. 6

18. (-3)

19. (-1)

20. (-5)

21. (-9)

22. 0

23. (-4)

24. 5

25. 0

26. 5

27. 1

28. 2

29. (-3)

30. 10

31. 9

32. (-10)

33. 0

34. (-4)

35. (-4)

36. (-3)

37. (-6)

38. 7

39. (-9)

40. 5

41. (-4)

42. 9

43. (-9)

44. 4

45. 2

46. 6

Mixed addition & subtraction of Integers

1. -26
2. 8
3. -15
4. 0
5. 7
6. -3
7. -10
8. 29
9. -16
10. -14
11. -3
12. -10
13. 3
14. 5
15. 4
16. -3
17. 4
18. 1
19. 16
20. -2
21. -20
22. 1
23. 2
24. 17
25. 28
26. -22
27. -1
28. -19
29. -5
30. 12
31. -1
32. -11

Integer Multiplication

1. -40
2. 171
3. 63
4. 144
5. -117
6. -11
7. 64
8. -22
9. -135
10. -135
11. 7
12. -22
13. -48
14. 5
15. 12
16. 50
17. -32
18. 24
19. -140
20. 51

Integer Division

1. 18
2. 50
3. 0
4. 11
5. 16
6. 11
7. 7
8. 8
9. 31
10. 9
11. 4
12. 6
13. -9
14. -2
15. 35
16. 13
17. 9
18. -10
19. 16
20. 16

11.621 84567LV00026B/1752 [430822748]

www.ingramcontent.com/pod-product-compliance
Lightning Source LLC
LaVergne TN